Every effort has been made to trace the author and
owner of the copyright of these prayers.
We offer our sincere apologies if we
have used copyright material
without due acknowledgement.

MY BOOK
of FAVORITE
PRAYERS

Illustrated by Linda Pasifull
Prayers originated and selected
by Marjorie Newman

AUGSBURG • MINNEAPOLIS

God's Love and care

Our Father hears us when we pray.
 A whisper can He hear.
He knows not only what we say
 But what we wish and fear.

John Barton, 1803-77

Thank You, God, because I can talk
to You anytime, anywhere. You will always listen.
You will help me. You love me.

M. Newman

With You beside me, Father God
 I journey on my way.
What need I fear when Thou art near,
 O King of night and day?

Saint Columba 521-597
(slightly adapted)

Into Your loving care,
Into Your keeping,
God who is everywhere,
Take us, we pray.

Traditional

HOME AND FAMILY

God bless all those that I love
God bless all those that love me.
God bless all those that love
those that I love, and all those
that love those who love me.

New England Sampler

You are our Father, God!
We are all part of Your family -
and You are part of ours!
Thank You, God!

M. Newman

We ask God's blessing on this house,
and all who live in it.
May its rooms be filled with kindness.
May love dwell within its walls,
and joy shine from its windows.

From 'Forms of Prayer for Jewish Worship'
© 1977 Reform Synagogues of Great Britain

Father God, sometimes we get really *cross*
with people in our family.
It makes us sad - and it makes You sad, too.
Help us to forgive one another
and be happy again,
the way You want us to be.

M. Newman

FRIENDS

Friends are fun, God!

Friends are for playing with,
laughing with, sharing with!

Friends are for talking to,
telling secrets to, listening to!

Sometimes, God, friends are for
quarrelling with...

Help us make up our quarrels quickly,
and to be good friends to one another.

Thank You for our friends.

M. Newman

Sometimes I'm lonely, God.

I stand by myself and watch
the other chidren playing together.
I *wish* I had a friend.

Please help me to find one, God!
Show me how to *be* friendly.

And when at last I have lots of friends,
help me to watch out for other children
who are still lonely.

Help me to make friends with them, too.

M. Newman

Help us to do the things we should,
  To be to others kind and good.
In all we do in work or play,
  To grow more loving every day.

Rebecca J. Weston, circa 1890

ME!

My tongue can taste all sorts of
things.
All kinds of things! So many things!
My nose can smell all sorts of things.
I thank You, Heavenly Father.

My ears can hear all sorts of
things.
All kinds of things! So many things!
My eyes can see so many things.
I thank You, Heavenly Father.

My hands can touch all sorts of
things.
All kinds of things! So many things!
And I can do so many things!
I thank You, Heavenly Father.

M. Newman

Lord of the loving heart,
May mine be loving too.

Anon

Holy God, who madest me
  Make me fit to worship Thee.
Fit to stand, fit to run,
  Fit for sorrow, fit for fun.
Fit for work, fit for play,
  Fit to face life every day.
Holy God, who madest me
  Make me fit to worship Thee.

Anon (slightly adapted)

I'm sad, God.
I want to cry.
I want to curl up small.
I want someone to come
and cuddle me.
You know all about it, God.
Please help me to feel better soon.

M. Newman

I'm angry, God!
I want to stamp!
I want to shout!
I want to punch the pillow!
I know You understand, God.
You know all about it, God.
Please help me to feel better soon.

M. Newman

When I'm happy and safe,
I'll remember to say,
"Please, God, let nothing
be hurt today."

Anon (adapted)

GRACES

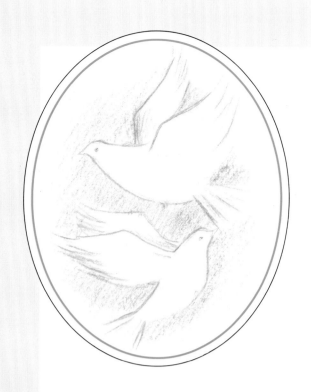

Thank You for the world so sweet,
Thank You for the food we eat.
Thank You for the birds that sing.
Thank You, God, for everything!

E. Rutter Leatham, 1870-1933

All good gifts around us
  Are sent from Heaven above.
Then thank the Lord, O thank the Lord
  For all His love!

Matthias Claudius, 1740-1815
(Translated by Jane Montgomery Campbell, 1817-78)

Father we thank Thee for the night,
  And for the pleasant morning light.
For rest and food, and loving care
  And all that makes the day so fair.

Rebecca J. Weston, circa 1890

Thanks to Thee, kind Father
  For my daily bread.
For my home and playthings.
  For my cozy bed.

Charles Arnold Healing, 1868-1921

ANIMALS

Creator, hear and bless
  Thy beasts and singing birds.
And guard with tenderness
  Small things that have no words.

Anon

Hey all you children,
Bless you the Lord!
All fathers and mothers,
Sisters and brothers,
Praise Him and magnify Him for ever!

All you deeps of the ocean,
Praise you the Lord!
All whales and porpoises,
Turtles and tortoises,
Praise Him and magnify Him for ever!

All field mice and larder mice,
Praise you the Lord!
All hedgehogs and voles,
Rabbits and moles,
Praise Him and magnify Him for ever!

Anon

Thank You, God, for pets to love.
Help us to find out what they need so
that they will be happy living with us.
And let us never forget they are
part of Your world - Your creation.

M. Newman

NIGHT TIME

Goodnight! Goodnight!
 Far flies the light.
 But still God's love
 Shall shine above,
 Making all bright.
Goodnight! Goodnight!

Victor Hugo (translation), 1802-85

Lord, when we have not any light,
 And mothers are asleep,
Then through the stillness
 of the night
Thy little children keep.

Annie Matheson, 1853-1924

Jesus, tender shepherd, hear me
 Bless Thy little lamb tonight.
Through the darkness be Thou near me,
 Keep me safe till morning light.

Mary Duncan, 1814-40

Glory to Thee my God this night
For all the blessings of the light.
Keep me, O keep me, King of Kings,
Beneath Thine own almighty wings.

Thomas Ken, 1637-1711

THE PRAYER JESUS TAUGHT US

Our Father,
Who art in Heaven
Hallowed be Thy name.
Thy Kingdom come,
Thy will be done,
On earth, as it is in Heaven.
Give us this day our daily bread
And forgive us our trespasses
As we forgive those who trespass
  against us.
And lead us not into temptation,
But deliver us from evil.
For Thine is the Kingdom,
The power and the glory,
For ever and ever, Amen.

Matthew 6: 9-13

Praise God from whom all
  blessings flow.
Praise Him, all creatures
  here below.

Thomas Ken, 1637-1711

NATURE

O God, open my eyes to what is beautiful,
My mind to know what is true,
My heart to love what is good,
For Jesus' sake, Amen.

Lutterworth Press

Creator God, who made the world,
we want to share in taking care of it.
May we never carelessly harm any living thing.
And may we always try to make the place
where *we* live a little bit more beautiful.
Thank You, God, for making the world!

M. Newman

We thank Thee, Lord, for this fair earth.
The glittering sky. The silver sea.

George Edward Lynch Cotton, 1813-66

Winter day! Frosty day!
God a cloak on all doth lay.
On the earth the snow He spreadeth.
Gives the bird a coat of feathers
To protect it from the weather.
Gives the children home and food.
Let us praise Him! God is good!

From 'Poems for Home Life'

CHRISTMAS

Loving God, thank you for Christmas!

Thank You for the presents we get because people love us!

Thank You for the people we give presents to because we love them!

Help us to notice people who are sad, so that we can try to make their Christmas happier.

And thank You very much for baby Jesus, Your gift of love to us.

M. Newman

Glory to God in the Highest,
And on earth, peace.
Goodwill towards men!

Luke 2:14

Wind through the olive trees
  Softly did blow
Round little Bethlehem,
  Long, long ago.

Sheep on the hillside lay,
  Whiter than snow,
Shepherds were watching them,
  Long, long ago.

Then from the happy sky
  Angels bent low
Singing their songs of joy,
  Long, long ago.

For in a manger bed
  Cradled, we know,
Christ came to Bethlehem,
  Long, long ago.

Thank You, Heavenly Father!

Anon

SPRING AND EASTER

For lo, the winter is past,
the rain is over and gone;
the flowers appear on the earth;
the time of the singing birds
is come.

Song of Solomon 2:11-12

Dear Jesus - on Good Friday we
remember You loved us so much,
You died for us on a cross.
It makes us sad that You had to die.
But on Easter morning we remember
You are alive again!
That makes us feel so glad!
Thank You, Lord Jesus.

M. Newman

The world itself keeps Easter Day,
  And Easter larks are singing
And Easter flowers bloom today
  And Easter buds are springing!

John Mason Neale, 1818-66
(slightly adapted)